Nature Walk
Leaves

by Rebecca Stromstad Glaser

J
575.57
E
GLA

POTTSTOWN PUBLIC LIBRARY
POTTSTOWN PA

Bullfrog
Books

Ideas for Parents and Teachers

Bullfrog Books let children practice reading informational texts at the earliest reading levels. Repetition, familiar words, and photo labels support early readers.

Before Reading
- Discuss the cover photo. What does it tell them?
- Look at the picture glossary together. Read and discuss the words.

Read the Book
- "Walk" through the book and look at the photos. Let the child ask questions. Point out the photo labels.
- Read the book to the child, or have him or her read independently.

After Reading
- Prompt the child to think more. Ask: What kinds of leaves have you seen? What kind of plants did they grow on?

Bullfrog Books are published by Jump!
5357 Penn Avenue South
Minneapolis, MN 55419
www.jumplibrary.com

Copyright © 2013 Jump! International copyright reserved in all countries. No part of this book may be reproduced in any form without written permission from the publisher.

Library of Congress Cataloging-in-Publication Data
Glaser, Rebecca Stromstad.
Leaves / by Rebecca Stromstad Glaser.
p. cm. -- (Bullfrog books: nature walk)
Summary: "Describing different types of leaves, this photo-illustrated nature walk guide shows very young readers how to identify common types of leaves. Includes picture glossary"--Provided by publisher.
Includes bibliographical references and index.
ISBN 978-1-62031-025-0 (hardcover)
Leaves--Juvenile literature. I. Title.
QK649.G53 2013
575.5'7--dc23   2012009100

Series Designer   Ellen Huber
Book Designer   Ellen Huber
Photo Researcher   Heather Dreisbach

Photo Credits: Dreamstime.com, 1c, 1r, 3t, 4, 5, 6, 8, 9b, 9t, 11, 13, 14, 15, 17, 20b, 21, 22, 23tl, 23bl, 24; Getty Images, 20b, 21; iStockphoto, 7, 12; Shutterstock, cover, 1l, 3b, 10, 16, 18-19, 20t, 23tr, 23br

Printed in the United States of America at Corporate Graphics in North Mankato, Minnesota
7-2012/PO 1123

10 9 8 7 6 5 4 3 2 1

Table of Contents

Looking for Leaves

Let's go on a nature walk.

Do you see leaves?

5

**Look for a birch leaf.
It is pointed.**

It turns yellow in fall.

Look for pine needles.

They stay green all year.

9

Look for
an elm leaf.

It has a
toothed edge.

leaflet

Look for an ash leaf.

It is compound.

A compound leaf has several leaflets.

13

Look for a fern.

It has compound leaves too.

15

Look for grass.

16

Its leaves are flat and narrow.

Look for a water lily.

Each flower has one round leaf.

Look for butterfly weed.
Each stem has many thin leaves.
Where do you see leaves?

Parts of a Leaf

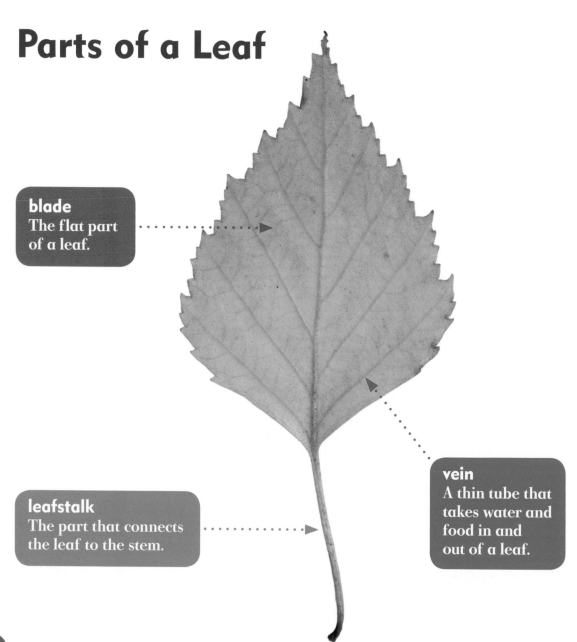

blade
The flat part of a leaf.

leafstalk
The part that connects the leaf to the stem.

vein
A thin tube that takes water and food in and out of a leaf.

Picture Glossary

compound leaf
A leaf in which several leaflets grow from one leaf stem.

needle
A thin, round, pointed leaf on a pine tree.

leaflet
A small leaf that is part of a compound leaf.

toothed
Jagged on the edges, like a saw blade.

Index

To Learn More

Learning more is as easy as 1, 2, 3.

1) Go to www.factsurfer.com

2) Enter "leaves" into the search box.

3) Click the "Surf" button to see a list of websites.

With factsurfer.com, finding more information is just a click away.